The Fine Art Of Getting Even

The Fine Art

Of

Getting Even

(A comical

Approach to

revenge)

By: R. D. Krause

The Fine Art Of Getting Even

ISBN: 9781977059710

<u>Disclaimer</u>

The author assumes no responsibility for the use or misuse of the ideas described. The author specifically disclaims any personal liability, loss or risk incurred as a consequence of the use, either directly or indirectly, of any information presented herein. This book comes with absolutely no warranty, in particular regarding the authenticity or accuracy of any action described herein.

All methods, actions and other data in this writing are meant for information purposes and mental exercise only and should not be attempted. Some of the schemes described in this book are illegal to perform, and all are immoral. Most of them will make your target suffer in one way or another.

You should consider this text as a source of amusement, not as a manual of how to create havoc and get yourself into trouble.

In other words, do not do this at home kids!

Remember, even if you do not get caught, Karma is a Bitch! Everything you say, do , and to some extent, think. Has a very nasty habit of coming back to you!

The Fine Art Of Getting Even

Dedication

This work is dedicated to all of those out there that have had the misfortune of having run afoul of the many ignorant, self-centered, uncaring, cretins that seem to populate our world in this day and age.

The Fine Art Of Getting Even

Foreword

For more years than I care to think about, several of my friends and associates have kiddingly said that I wrote the book on evil, wicked, mean, and nasty. They have asked me when I was going to write all of my evil tricks down and share them with the world. Usually, during an evening of indulgents while consuming massive quantities of Rocky Mountain Silver Bullets assisted by that notorious Pirate Captain.

In the six and a half decades I have been on this ball of dirt we call the Earth. I have had a few occasions when I have run afoul of certain other individuals for one reason or another and have had the thought of dastardly revenge and payback, come sweetly to my mind. It has been during those moments of pain and disappointment that I have developed the methods and schemes approached in this work.

Then several months ago, while sitting and talking to my three best friends, Lexi Lu, Aesop, and Kodiak, my three pups. I proposed the idea of actually writing a work on the subject. I decided that I wanted to compose it as a comical approach to getting even, revenge and payback. They seemed to agree that it would be a good idea, or at less they did not disagree. That of course may have had something to do with the treats I had in hand at the time. At any rate we decided that at the very least it would relieve the boredom of being old, broke and depressed!

And that is how the project got started. I am very happy to say that now in the winter of my life, that I have not enacted many of the schemes laid out in this

The Fine Art Of Getting Even

work. Not, mind you because they do not work. But rather because I have an extremely healthy respect for Karma! I have learned in my sixty five years of life that everything is on the wheel. Everything you say, do, or enact, be it good, bad, or indifferent will at some point come back to you in one way or another. With that being said, please enjoy the read and have fun. Hopefully few of you will ever indulge yourselves in more than the planning stage.

Have fun, be careful, and be smart.

The

Author

Table of contents

Foreword   7
 Contents   9
Chapter 1   10
Chapter 2   13
Chapter3   17
Chapter 4   22
Chapter 5   27
Chapter 6   31
Chapter 7   41
Chapter 8   50
Chapter 9   56
Chapter 10   58
Chapter 11   68
Chapter 12   82
Chapter 13   86
Chapter 14   91
 Epilogue / Also Know AsThe End   111

Chapter 1 / Planning

So, hello all of you out there that have been put upon, snubbed, downgraded, cheated on, overlooked or just plain shit on. By some self-satisfying, inconsiderate jackass that thinks his shorts do not stink.

In the pages of this manuscript we will attempt to show you how you may be able to teach this asshole a lesson or two. Or at least get some satisfaction from returning the pain you have had to its source.

Now we all know that you are an angel and would never do anything wrong.

But every so often even the best of us has a run in with some evil wrong doer that thinks they have the right to treat us as if we do not matter.

It may have been a coworker or a boyfriend or a husband, or even heaven forbid a girlfriend or wife. Or it might be a neighbor, brother, cousin, aunt, uncle, shopkeeper, waitress or waiter, or even a customer.

In today's society it could be almost anyone. We are all subject to misuse by others that really have no right consuming oxygen. It is the sign of the times. It is these dastardly individuals that bring out the devil in all of us.

Most of the time, we just ignore these cretins and go on with our life as if nothing has happened. But, sometimes the affront has been so damaging that we are unable to let it go.

Those are the times when we decide that we have to do something.

The first thing we have to remember is that any action needs a plan. Failing to plan is the same thing as planning to fail.

One of the biggest mistakes that most people make is that they try to retaliate when they are mad. Do not get mad, instead get even!

The next mistake that many make is the belief that it is necessary to let the subject of you wrath know that his/her come-up-pence is on its way to their doorstep. Always remember that revenge is a dish best served cold!

The less your enemy knows about what you plan the better. You know why, what is about to befall him/her is all about. They do not need too. Let it be a surprise, you will enjoy it more, and it will keep them wondering what just flipping hit them.

After all they did not warn you when they did the dastardly deed to you that caused you to decide to seek revenge. Did they?

Chapter 2 /Phase 1 /The Recon

So okay here we go. Are you sure you want to do this? Remember Newton's Law of Motion is in effect in all things.

"For every action there is an equal and opposite reaction."

Yes, Grasshopper, we are talking Science here!

Now every good Pot-Metal General knows that the secret to a good battle plan is massive amounts of good and accurate

information about the other guy.

It is possible that you already know everything there is to know about the subject of your wrath. Such as where he or she lives, where they work, what they like to eat or drink, what kind of car they drive or do not drive. If they like cats or dogs (note: You can tell a lot about a person with this information). But, most likely not, after all if you knew that much about them you would not have allowed yourself to be taken in. Would you have?

For the sake of argument, let us say you do not know that much about the scum sucking, bottom feeding, worm that has done you wrong.

In fact you barely know him, her, them at all. They just popped into your life and screwed with you!

So how do we get the poop on him, find the skivvy, dig up the dirt, and unbury the skeletons? Have no fear Grasshopper, I am about to enlighten you on the art of discovery. We will now begin the recon phase! Get ready to start digging. Dastardly Dan has no secrets that you cannot find and use to bring his funky butt down. Let the games begin.

Now in this phase of the operation you will have to use some new skills. You are going to learn how to use Social Engineering and Role Camouflage.

In today's times everyone has an online profile. Except for those few people who have worked very hard to stay under the radar so to speak. This in itself tells you a lot about that person.

So the first place we will start looking for information on Dastardly Dan is on the web.

The Fine Art Of Getting Even

Do not use your home computer if you can help it. Go to the Library and use theirs. Secrecy and stealth is the key here. Later on when the Veri-Grow hits the Mix Master, we do not what someone to be able to trace back and find out who done it!

You want to check out Facebook, LinkedIn, My Space, and other Social media sites. You can find out an awful lot about someone by checking these sites out. Such as, their habits, location, home town, birthday, friends, business, hobbies and such other trivially things.

It is amazing how much personal information people put on social media sites, for the world to see!

Next if you have found out where he works check out his company's website. This will usually give you some insight on the way the company works and usually, who the big muckity-mucks are, with such things as their phone numbers, email addresses and stuff.

Next do a Google Search on Mr. Wonderful and see what comes up. Check the County Court records, and the Arrest records.

So okay before we go any further let's lay down the ground rules that should help to keep you safe.

So far everything we have done has been nonintrusive and relatively untraceable. From this point on let it here by and here on, be known that, Mr. Wonderful, Dastardly Dan, Little Miss Diva, Ditsy Darlene shall be known as The Mark. It saves on time and decreases confusion.

Chapter 3 / Planning and Safety

The typical lifecycle of a revenge scheme often starts with someone, a person or a member of an organization, doing something wrong to you, or someone close to you.

At that moment you, the victim, would most likely be in a state of anger, hate or sadness. At least you should be in a state where you wish to get even at the one, or the ones, who wronged you.

The worst thing that could happen at this moment is that you sharpen your swords of vengeance and go on right at it.

Revenge done in haste is such a waste, and the Sicilians did really know what they were talking about when they were saying,

"Revenge is a dish best served cold."

It is time to sit back, heal your wounds and start plotting your payback. This could take months, or even years, depending on how severe the offense was and how severe you want the payback to be.

It wouldn't surprise me if 50% of the avengers who get caught are people who start their mission of vengeance at a time that is too close to the crime.

I would also guess that 40% of the ones, who get caught, did not act out of a plan. Or they planned it badly without thought or skill. Then the rest,10% are the ones who simply get unlucky, where the unknown plays a factor that is not calculable. Murphy's Law is real Grasshopper. The simple fact is that anything that can go wrong usually will and that Mother Nature is a Bitch.

The life-span of a general revenge scheme should therefore start with the offense, continue with a great deal of patience, evolve through thorough planning and reconnaissance, reconsidered, and if necessarily some more patience, until you one day deploy your plan.

After that you have hopefully gotten your vengeance, and then everything related to this should be burned, buried and forgotten.

Remember to always stay flexible, be ready to change directions at a moment's notice. And always have a plan "B"!

Or after all the planning you may very well decide to forget it, that it really is not worth the effort or risk.

One different way of handling this is to make a list of all your Marks. This list could be something as direct as a little notebook with names, addresses, their crime and any other relevant and irrelevant pieces of information. Or you may decide to create a small data base on your computer, just remember to encrypt it and after the attack totally destroy it so it does not come back to haunt you.

Every now and then you get your list, fill in some gaps and delete obsolete data.

Then when the right time comes you seem to strike out of nowhere and before the Mark knows what hit him, you are gone again.

An advantage of this approach is that you can play several Marks against each other, and you could sit on

The Fine Art Of Getting Even

 your list for years, making your Marks less suspicious and unaware. There might also be times when you really want your Mark to know who you are. This would be in situations where you're participating in a direct revenge, or prank-war. This is a situation where nobody wins and should be avoided at all costs. Still, if you entangle yourself into this kind of situation, make sure that your Mark can't document any threats or actions done by you, as these cases tend to end up in a courthouse.

Electronic evidence and plans should be carefully encrypted, or better yet, destroyed completely; it might get used against you. Also be aware of the fact that these types of wars have the tendency of escalating to a point where things really get out of hand. The best way is the safe way, without much chance of retaliation and detection.
Patience, persistence, planning, and then finally the realization.
After the patience comes planning, and with planning comes surveillance.

Every fact and every detail about your Mark should be gathered and organized. The more you know about your Mark, the better. This involves information about his home and work address, telephone number, email address, habits, bank accounts, his social security number, wife, lovers, children, his fear, what he likes, dislikes, car license plate, daily and weekly routines, hobbies, religion, etc.

When all the pieces are gathered, you'll have a concept of who your Mark is, and you may then determine which of the many ways to get back at him would be the most efficient. This is where your plan forms and it should include all the "what, when and how's" that you can come up with.

The plan should also have contingency plans that describe how to act if you're exposed, and how to act if your Mark or the authorities confronts you later with your deeds.

Still, no-matter how well you have planned and executed your revenge scheme, there's always the chance that you'll end up among the 10% unlucky ones.

One friend of mine once said, "Be prepared to do the time for the crime," and indeed, if you can't afford getting caught, then you shouldn't do anything at all. All around the world there are people in prison, people who thought they would never get caught, some of which are very smart.

Chapter 4/ A few things to always keep in mind

Here are a few things to always keep in mind:

Never use your own telephone. Why? Because, your target can then track you with ease. It really only takes a caller-id and most people have those. Also,the telephone companies could be logging all the calls that we make.

(If you don't believe that watch the movie "The President's Analysis", also we know that "No Such Agency" is and has been monitoring the telephone lines here in the home of the free for years.)

Use a phone booth away from your vicinity and the path where you usually travel. If you can even find one anymore. Buy a "burner" cell phone at Seven Eleven or some such place and register it under a fake name. Go on EBAY and get a lineman's test set butt phone.

Never drive to your Mark's house with your own car. People you know might see it, and later when your

Mark asks questions, it may surface again. Also never use a Taxi, instead use public transport like a bus to an area close to the Mark's house and then walk the rest of the way.

Never work with your bare hands uncovered. Even if you have never been fingerprinted in the past, such as for a military service, there is no guarantee that this luxury will continue. Wear gloves instead, but don't throw them away at the crime scene or you may be forced to try them out in a courtroom. Ask a certain football player about that one!

The Fine Art Of Getting Even

Never let anyone see you. This might sound obvious, but wearing dark colored clothes at night might be a good idea. Not necessarily black as that also sticks out like a sore thumb. It is hard to distinguish dark colors at night. But Law Enforcement is usually on the lookout for black. Just don't stand out too much from your surroundings. Sometimes dressing casual might be better than dressing dark, and camouflage gear is definitely out of the question.

Never talk to anyone about what you have done. If someone confronts you with the issue, act ignorant. This is where many people fail and get caught. They have a trusted friend, who has a trusted friend, who has a trusted friend, etc. Old Ben Franklin said it best when he stated,

"Yes three people can keep a secret. But only if two of them are dead!*"*.

Never steal, anything unless you plan to throw it into a river before you get home. It would be real hard to explain if someone found an object belonging to your Mark at your place after he has had a break in.

Never use your own handwriting or your own printer or typewriter. Even if you try to forge the handwriting it is possible that they might trace it back to you. A printer or a typewriter will also have its own characteristics, often there is a character with certain distinction due to wear and tear. The best thing is to use one at a university, a school or one that is otherwise publicly accessible.

Never use saliva on stamps and envelopes.
DNA analysis is now a fact of life. People have been convicted because they did this.
Water from the spring or facet will do just fine.
Never involve an accomplice, unless it is absolutely necessary. The fewer who know about your work, the better it is. Even if that other person is someone you trust with your life, it still increases the risk when more people know about it.

Never threaten your Mark. If you threaten your Mark then he knows you'll be up to something. He'll also know where to start looking when something has happened and what names to fill in under suspicious persons in the entry box of a police report.

Never mail a letter from or near your home, city/town, workplace, etc. Use a re-mailer-service instead, or a trusted friend from out of town. Or better still take a short trip on a weekend to another town and mail your stuff from there.
Never buy supplies from a local dealer, and never use your credit card or check in the purchase. These are obvious, but unfortunately easy to forget when you don't plan things thoroughly. Remember cash has no memory!

 Never leave written documentation, like name, address, etc. at a place where it may be found. If you are storing such information on your computer, then make sure to encrypt it first. Or better yet put all of the data on an encrypted thumb drive that can be erased, smashed, and burnt when you are done. Remember that anything you do on the Internet is there FOREVER!! And can be traced, be careful!

These precautions might seem a bit paranoid, but I would be willing to bet that about 90% of everyone who ever gets caught didn't pay enough attention to planning or one of the precautions above. Some of the tactics in this book might break some of the rules above, but then again you are allowed to use your own head to evaluate the risk. After all, when it comes right down to it and the rubber hits the road. You are the one who will pay the penalty for failure!

Chapter 5 / The Camouflage

So now you have done your electronic recon, you have learned everything you could about your Mark by previewing his Facebook and LinkedIn pages and have delved into his history at his workplace through the Company's webpage. You have discovered who his friends are and where he likes to hang out. You now know where he lives and what kind of car he drives. And it has only taken you three weeks or so of going to different Libraries and Universities using their computers to discover all of these things but you still need to get more!

The time has come for that Role Camouflage I mentioned earlier.
It is a sad fact that in our society the average citizen ignores the homeless and unwashed masses. And the upper crust avoids them like the plague. So, that my friend, is going to be our disguise for this part of the recon.

Now the first thing we are going to do is to go to several Thrift stores and pick up a couple of things. We are going to pay cash for our items and we are not going to buy more than two or three things at any one store.

The Fine Art Of Getting Even

We need a big jacket with big pockets like an old
military field jacket, the more worn and ragged the
better. We need a dark colored shirt and a pair of
ragged pants like blue jeans or something along those
lines. We need a scruffy backpack and a pair of beat
up shoes. Also, we need a pair of gloves, again the
scruffier the better, and an old flop hat. Don't spend a
lot on these things as we will be re-donating them into
a drop box or two when we are done with this part of
the recon.
Heck, look in the dumpster behind the store you
might find everything you need there.

Once we have our disguise we are
going to make it even better by
soaking it all in some mild
ammonia water and throwing them
in the dirt in the back yard. We
want them to be dirty and smell bad
so now we are going to put the lot
into a plastic garbage bag and let
them sit in the bottom of a closet for about a week.
By then they should be pretty rank!
During the curing period we are going to go around to
the different bars and restaurants and pick up about a
half a garbage bag full of old empty beer cans. And
maybe a beat up old folding cart or one of those
suitcases that are on wheels, like you see the Yuppy
masses pulling around at the airports. Just make sure
it is scruffy not new.
While we are at the Thrift Store we also want to try
and pick up a few other things that we may need at a
later date. Such as a yellow or white construction

hardhat, some work shirts and pants, the one that have a company logo on them, maybe a pair of work boots, an old tool belt and pouch, some dark sunglasses, a clipboard. That sort of things.

Our next objective is to don our disguise and become a Bag Guy or Lady. We are going to peruse our Mark's garbage can or dumpster at his/her home and work. We are looking for bank statements, cancelled checks, credit card bills or offers, anything that might have his/her account numbers, routing numbers, etc.

Okay breathe, it has been a tough job but now we have everything we can dig up on the Mark. We know where he/she works, we know what time he/she goes to work and when he/she gets home, we know where they hang out on their off time, we know where they bank, eat, sleep, play. We have their phone numbers, bank and credit card numbers, routing numbers.

We know what their habits are who their friends are and what kind of food they like to eat we even know what kind of toilet paper they use. We have samples of his / her DNA from the cigarette butts and hair we pick out of their garbage can.

Basically we know the Mark better than they do themselves.

We have all the data and information we need to plan and execute a concentrated attack in an attempt to totally destroy their lives.

The Recon is over!

Take a break and unwind, relax go to diner, catch a show.

The Mark doesn't know it but his/her life has just changed forever!

Next we formulate the Plan!

Chapter 6 / The Plan

At this point we need to decide just how badly we want to get back at the Mark. Do we just want to cause him / her a little bit of discomfort or do we want to completely destroy him / her?

Long Distant Revenge

When your Mark doesn't live in your vicinity, there are two channels for you to use. The first is the old classical postal system.

The other is any electronic wire, like a telephone or a computer network.

Danger of detection

The danger of being detected while using one of these channels increases with how advanced the technology is. This basically means that the old postal system is the safest and easiest to use, and that everything that is being done on a computer network, like the Internet, is being log-filed; and unless you're a wizard, you're most likely to be detected, tracked and caught.

Telephone precautions

Using the telephone might seem like a safe channel, as you could be sitting on the other side of the planet, plotting, preparing and executing your revenge. Do

not be fooled by this distance as it takes no more than a caller-ID to give away your identity. The first rule of long distance telephone revenge is therefore to use a pay phone which isn't located too close to where you live, work or travel.

You should never call the Mark directly; at least if he was a close friend or someone you have seen or talked too often. Change your voice with a piece of cloth, or a voice-scrambler which you can get on Ebay for around ten bucks from SpyGear. Any machine manipulation though helps very little. If the conversation is being recorded it is then often possible to reverse the manipulation. The only good solution to this is to involve a third party, preferably a secondary Mark who you can call, posing as the primary Mark.

You might also use a trusted friend (remember that trust is a fleeting thing!) to make the call to your Mark, but remember the more people that know what you are doing the higher your chances of getting caught are.

The mail system

One of the most classic, non-creative, ways of getting even through the mail system is by using those rip-out order forms found in commercial catalogues and magazines. Pull out the card and ask for information, order a product or subscribe to the magazine.

All you need to know is the Mark's name and address and within a few minutes of work you'll be able to help him receive tons of annoying paper. You might want to use his business address. So the stuff goes to his or her work place. Bosses just love this sort of thing. You, could also use this method to help him buy "bill me later" goods. This isn't considered revenge art but still one scheme that has worked for thousands over the years.

Empty messages have Power!

A different approach, one which has a psychological touch, is to send your Mark empty envelopes. Make them arrive from different locations with different handwriting over a period of, say, 2-3 years.
There are many variations to this tactic. You could, for instance, send the envelope opened, indicating that someone is stealing his mail.
You could include a single piece of paper with words like "DEATH!", "LIAR!", "THIEF!" or whatever seems appropriate. The idea here is not to threaten the Mark directly, but to remind him of what he is. Just don't write anything that might expose you as the originator of the messages.

How to Annoy non-smokers.

One thing that you can do if you are sending a letter to someone who isn't a smoker is to include cigarette ashes in the envelope. This fuels the fire caused by any rude or annoying letter.

Forged letters

Forging letters in other people's name is illegal, but as long as you never get caught, is there really anything to worry about?
Now for some examples using The Mark's forged name and address.

Send a letter to your nation's customs department

Asking for a permit to import narcotics. You ought to write this out with information saying that you have been a drug addict for a long time, and that you can't afford buying it on the street anymore. Write that it is for personal use only. It would even be better if your Mark really is a drug abuser.

Send a letter to the local church

Where you ask about the Christian view on sex with children. Tell them that you've read the bible, but that you couldn't find anything there stating that it is wrong.
Also state that you're trying to quit, but that the temptations are hard to handle.

Send a letter to his landlord

Telling him or her that you'll be moving shortly. Give the landlord a specific date, and tell him that you will be on vacation until a few days before the move. If you're lucky, the landlord might start

looking for new tenants without even confronting your Mark.
This is also a great scheme if the landlord is a secondary Mark.

Browse the job Market

Then apply for positions in your Mark's name. Give his new employer all sorts of peculiar, suspicious or incredible references, as if he has been working in your country's leading positions and attending at the best Universities. The objective is to have the employer go checking those references, as if these references don't add up, This could certainly cause legal problems for your Mark. Use the Mark's business address for the return address.

Apply for membership in certain groups

Something like the KKK, Jehovah's Witnesses, NAMBLA (North American Men and Boy Love Association), or anything controversial. If nothing else happens it might cause a red flag to go up at the offices of certain government agencies that monitor that sort of thing. Or subscribe him/her to annoying book clubs like the Reader's Digest. Find something the Mark really hates or fears and sign him up there.

Apply for credit cards, etc.

You will probably need your Mark's social security number to do this. But hopefully you got it when you were doing your Recon dumpster/garbage can diving.

The Fine Art Of Getting Even

You will not be able to use them, it's just that it will really make him wonder when he hasn't applied for the credit cards and they start arriving in the mail. With any kind of luck he / she may start using them and get in over their head as far as credit goes. It might even make him think that someone is working a scheme to abuse them, but that it is somehow failing.

Get an address change form

These are found at the post office. Make his new address somewhere isolated, or have it forwarded to any known criminal at the State Prison.

Write a letter to the reader's section of his local newspaper

Or maybe the university newspaper. You'll have to customize the letter to fit the crime, but you could do anything from complaining about his boss/ company to writing something that would be considered inappropriate with his friends.

Sending letters to your Mark from a secondary Mark
This might also work nicely. A computer and a scanner are all you need to copy off and make fake letterheads. The original letterhead can often be retrieved by sending the secondary Mark a simple inquiry about something trivial, and then scan the letter head from the reply note.

Use a work or campus computer to print out the letter.

The Fine Art Of Getting Even

Write a letter from your Mark's bank to your Mark

Saying that his whole loan is due if he has a loan, you should have found this out during your Recon and that he has to pay it back immediately, or they will go to court. You ought to come up with some clever reason, for instance that another company has bought the bank, and that they're now in the process of closing the business. Date the letter a few weeks back before sending it, and time it to arrive on a Saturday.

Write a letter from the local hospital or Health Department

Asking your Mark to come in for a checkup. Explain that a client with AIDS has named him as a past sexual partner. Name a doctor at the hospital, which should be a secondary Mark, and tell your main Mark that he should just come over as soon as possible.

Send him a letter from magazines like Playboy or Playgirl or Gay Life

Thanking him for the photographs he sent them to the reader's Husbands/Wives section. This is a good scheme to play out on an ex, where you also could send the letter from a magazine that's not easy to find in your area.

Send a letter from his teacher to his parents

The Fine Art Of Getting Even

If your Mark is still in school, describing him as a hopeless problem child. This could be implemented nicely if the teacher is a secondary Mark, where you would write that you, the teacher, would like their boy to be at school after school-time, because you feel that you are so close to him, and that you feel that you can communicate really well with him. The teacher would be sounding like a really strange one, and the kid would be left with councilors.

Write a letter from the local tax collector

Where you question his ability to buy a new cabin cruiser with as little as he earns. Demand that he explain this, and why the same cabin cruiser isn't on his tax report. Write that there most likely will be an investigation, and ask him to come over to the office at a specific date.

Write a letter from the local TV station
Telling your Mark that he has won a $12,000 car. Tell him to meet at the TV station at a specific time, like a late Saturday evening, for an interview.

The Fine Art Of Getting Even

Junk mail

Junk mail can be pretty annoying. It's a good thing that there's plenty of stuff to do with the reply-envelope, though. Just remember to remove any references like your name, address and customer identification before you do anything. Abuse of business reply envelopes is a violation of postal service regulations in nearly all countries throughout the world.

Junk mail and glue.

Glue some pieces of paper together. Put them into the reply-envelope and glue the entire envelope together. This sounds pretty harmless, but just imagine the poor fellow trying to pull that sucker open without tearing it.

Cross-mail your junk mail.

Just take company A's order-form and swap it with company B's junk mail. This makes great fun when you swap the porn catalogue with the local church's request for donations.

Mail revenge warning

I must urge you to please keep in mind that most of the mail scenarios are illegal in most countries. In fact, they're a federal offense in some cases, punishable by stiff fines and jail sentences. If you choose to do it anyway, use a mailbox located far

away from your house, perhaps in a neighboring city
or town that has a different post office.

The larger the city, or town is, and the further from
your own residence, the better. Also keep in mind not
to use your own saliva to lick the stamps, and do not
get fingerprints on letters or envelopes. Conceal your
handwriting as well or better still use a publicly
available typewriter or printer. Read the precautions
section carefully before commencing revenge by
mail.

Chapter 7 / The Telephone

There are certainly several critical aspects about using the telephone in revenge schemes. I have already mentioned these in the previous safety section, but since I feel these are important issues, I'll keep nagging about them, like I did in the last paragraph in the previous chapter.

Precautions ad tedium

The first issue is to never forget that there are many people who have caller-id on their telephone, that there's always a risk of being recognized by the person on the other side, and that he could be recording your conversation.

If you're calling from a pay phone using a slightly different accent than the one you use every day, talking through a device that changes your voice and use gloves or a cover when touching the pay phone, then you should be fairly safe.

Or you could get a lineman's butt phone test set from EBAY for around twenty bucks and use any line that you can get access to at the box where it comes into the house. You will want to use some sort of disguise like a hard hat, and tool belt and be dressed in work cloths so if someone sees you use the pay phone or Butt phone at that specific moment, they will not wonder who is using the phone, with all that equipment.

 When the Mark knows your voice, it would be safer to have a trusted friend (good luck finding one!) lend you his voice, or involve a secondary Mark who doesn't know your voice.

Basics

The most basic way of getting even by using the phone system is to call a business and pretend you're the Mark, and then order something from them. This could be a pizza restaurant, any magazine (Subscription), hotel (order rooms), travel agency (order tickets) or someone who could be delivering gravel at your Mark's house, preferably when your Mark is on a vacation. The downside about these tactics is that you'll be involving a third party, and since your Mark could just deny ordering a pizza, the loss would be on the shoulders of that innocent person or company and not your Mark.
Still, if you have any secondary Marks, like if you were wronged by a travel agency, this kind of tactic could be appropriate. There are variations of this tactic that might be more effective.

Stopping supplies

You could call the company that supplies gas or electricity to your Mark and tell them to shutdown the gas/electricity supply. The best time to do this is at a Friday morning or noon. When your Mark returns from work that evening he'll be greeted with a house without electric power, and the best part is that he won't have any until the electric-workers return to work after the weekend.

To complete this last one, call the phone company and have his phone shutdown, tell them he is moving. Also call his ISP (Internet Service Provider) and tell them that you won't need their services anymore. Cancel all his magazine/newspaper subscriptions and then call his credit card issuer and tell them that his card was stolen, impersonating him. You may get questions about birth date, address and such, so be prepared before you make the call.

Phone terrorism

The next level of payback by using the phone is much similar to the old telephone harassment. There are still ways to exert this in a creative way without becoming as boring as the call-your-Mark-and hang-up schemes. One way of doing this is to simply call your Mark.

Let it ring once or twice and then hang up. Do this randomly, day or night for increased effect. When the Mark is asleep he'll wake up just long enough to not get a stable good night's sleep. At days he might even get annoyed enough to call the phone company, thinking that something is wrong with his phone.

A different approach is to call your Mark in the middle of night, about 0500 am and pretend to be a hyperactive Tele-Marketer who is selling encyclopedias. Pretend that you're calling from a different time zone, and if he confronts you with the time in his zone then just carry on with the sale. If he wants the number to your boss, either give him the

number to a secondary Mark or the number to a police chief in the appropriate time zone. This works great when your Mark is a salesman who has somehow wronged you.

Wakeup calls

Wakeup calls are often used by pranksters, but they also make good use in light revenge schemes. The problem is just how to make the order call as some of the services require that you call from the some phone you want a wakeup at. At present, in the US, you can go to a web page, **www.mrwakeup.com** and order a wakeup call. This web-page may be down when you read this, but there are always other alternatives. The same goes for fax-back services found at **www.intellifax.com** and I am sure various other web-pages. Just remember that the services provided may log your IP and track the request back to you.

Collect calls

Another way of dealing with real long distance revenge is to call your Mark collect, pretending to be his father or mother, sister, or brother. Give the operator his relative's name and when you're connected, cough and grumble or just try to not expose who you are until some time has passed. This one is a bit tricky, but it might have the double effect that it hurts the Mark's phone-bill in addition to making him worry about whether his relative is alright or not.

Obscure calls

It's also really fun to just call your Mark in the middle of the night, pretending that it is he who is calling you. Act confused, act tired, act annoyed and cranky. Threaten to report him to the police and finally slam the phone down. Spontaneity is a key factor here.

Making "appointments"

In situations where you have a trusted friend at your side, the number of plays increases, especially if your friend is of the opposite sex from your Mark, and that friend has a good imagination and great skills in acting.

A date?

One thing a friend could help you do is call your Mark, tell him that she had seen him somewhere and that she (or he) would like to date him. Of course your friend would never meet at the date, but if you manage to play the Mark, then he will.

Implied adultery or unfaithfulness

When the Mark lives with a spouse or a girlfriend you, or your trusted accomplice, could call her up when you know he won't be there.
When the spouse picks up the phone, present yourself. When she has given her name, you proceed by telling her that you're his (the Mark's) girlfriend/fiancée and that she must be his sister. Continue without letting her interrupt by saying that the Mark is such a good guy who takes care of her. Act surprised when she tells you who she is. Explain that it must be a misunderstanding, that you've dated him for quite some time.
This requires that you have some time and locations where you were supposed to be together with him, and that you'll have to survey him a bit in advance. Also be ready to answer tricky questions, such as personal questions about the Mark. Just don't give his new love your real name.

The Fine Art Of Getting Even

The idea is to make your Mark's spouse
suspect that something is going on
between you and your Mark. To
increase the paranoia that this scheme
could cause, start calling them at
random times and just hang-up the phone if it is
answered.

Variations

You could also pose as the Mark's former gay lover,
actually there are a lot of ways to do this since these
tactics works in both directions. It all depends a bit on
how much you know the person you're supposed to be
with, and how well your Mark knows you or your
friend's voice.

Pagers

Pagers are also fun to play with. Just page your Mark
and leave another pager number. Leave his own
telephone number or leave the phone number of his
boss, a local drug dealer, the local police chief or
some 800-number phone sex line. Page secondary
Marks and have them call your primary Mark and
vice versa.

Fax machines

There are also things that you can do with a fax
machine. Just remember most fax machines print their
telephone numbers on the top page of the page they're
sending. I advise to you check on this first, unless

you're in a situation where you want the Mark to know who are sending him the garbage, or you are borrowing the fax at an office where they don't know you.

Infinite faxes

One known way to exploit faxes is to make an eternal loop by gluing the end of the fax paper to the start of it. Call the Mark's company and let the fax run for a whole weekend. You can also create a single piece of paper with the text ;

System Error 1207: Internal controller Failure

Then, make another paper with the text;

Disconnect the machine and contact qualified repair personnel

Send both pages, or loop them, on a late Friday afternoon and hope that they'll go for it.

Big companies

When your Mark works at a big company then it is likely that someone will read or at least have a look at the fax for sorting purposes. Send your Mark a page with a big heart from his lover of the opposite of his sexual preference.

The Fine Art Of Getting Even

Black magic

An old fax trick is to loop completely black pages to your Mark's fax. And then send to a company fax machine that he works with, preferable on a weekend when they are closed.

This trick is particularly nasty to play on old thermal-paper faxes, which might even be ruined by the heat caused by only printing black some have even been known to catch on fire due to the heat generated by this. Other fax machines will spit out paper and ink worth many dollars.

Chapter 8 / The Internet

The Internet is one of the most difficult arenas to carry out safe long distance revenge. The reason for this is that everything that is being done is being log-filed.

Regarding logging

If you log in on your net account, then there's a program that writes information about who you are and when you login, into a file. When you access a web-page, then the web-server logs the time and your computer's address.
The same goes for every kind of Internet service, they all keep a log. This is done so that they can trace any connection back to the originator.

Basics
One secure way of getting even through the net, is by using a computer where you don't have to

give away your login name and password, and where nobody can confirm that you were at the terminal, behind that keyboard at that specific time. This situation becomes real when you're at a public terminal at a library, or in an Internet café where nobody knows you or can prove that you're at the terminal at the specific time.

There are also some limitations on carrying out your revenge from a library computer. One is that you can't access programs that you normally would have on your system, unless the library gives access to disks, which they rarely do for security reasons. If you try to grab something out of your own account or web-page, then it will be logged and things could be traced back to you. The tools that you most often are limited to are therefore a WWW-client, Telnet and FTP. Knowledge in using and understanding how these tools work is essential.

Another problem with the net is that things change at an incredible pace. Things that seem obvious and easy today will most likely change even before this book is released. This is really why I would not recommend newbies to try to get even through the net.

Now for a few ideas.

Internet revenge ideas

The Fine Art Of Getting Even

The first thing you need to do, as said, is getting access to a publicly available computer without giving away your identity. When this is  done, you may enter the web-browser configuration, changing the name and email to the one of your Mark. This will lead newbies to believe that it is your Mark who is at the console, the more advanced Internet users will recognize the difference.

The next thing to do might be to put out a few contact ads with your Mark's name, address and phone numbers on. Use every source available like alt.sex.wanted and alt.personals on the Internet.

 On the web there are many contact ad sites. You should save time by finding these sites and others in advance, and writing them onto a piece of paper. When forging contact ads in his name becomes boring, try selling stuff in the Market groups or through appropriate web-walls.

There are many places on the net where you can leave his name and E-mail address for subscriptions on things like magazines and web-page updates. Search the net for a little while and you will easily find such services. The nice thing about mailing lists is that the Mark would have to go searching through a lot of text to find out how to unsubscribe from them.

One way to give your Mark a lot of negative attention is to just be obnoxious on the net. You can start spamming (posting commercial ads or make money fast schemes) to various newsgroups or you can behave like a real obnoxious asshole (flaming). There is still a chance that this might not have any effect, as there are many idiots out there already. A different approach might be needed.

Send an email to his system-administrator where you write that he will no longer be in need of his Internet account anymore. Don't forget to mention the bad service you've been getting and that a slow feed is mainly the reason for changing ISP. E-mail requests to various other

ISP's requesting prices, ask for a subscription.

Dealing with Internet harassment

There are many people who have experienced being harassed on the Internet.

This often becomes very frustrating, especially if you're a newbie and don't know how things work. Oldtimers such as myself, often don't want to teach you anything; they just want you to go away, so that you can't bother them with your simple questions. This is, of course, dependent on what environment you operate in, but in general, you'll experience it as something really tough to fight, because you'll never see or hear the offender. Of course your Mark will run into the same problem. If by some chance he is the recipient. Which, by the way, can work out for you if, you are the offender!

All that you will see is a cryptic message header, which doesn't really say much to someone who hasn't got a clue. So, what can you do?

The Fine Art Of Getting Even

When you receive an abusive message, it being through electronic mail or in any Usenet group, the first thing you should do is to try to figure out as much as you can about the sender. Save the message, with the complete header, or print it out if necessary. If you think that the origin of the message is clear, then you could forward the whole message (with all headers intact) to the offender's system administrator. If you have gotten into your Mark's computer by some strange chance and sent yourself those messages from him all the better.

The system administrator has email addresses like abuse@(domain), postmaster@(domain) and support@(domain).

Reporting the abuse

If you have a chance to get into your Mark's computer. You could send the afore mentioned abusive message to yourself from his /her computer. After that has been done.

You should report the abuse to the police. They love that sort of thing these days. It gives them a chance to go in and seize everything the Mark has that is electrical.

If he / she is a student you can report him / her to the Dean of Student Affairs.

If by some strange chance it makes references to your race, ethnicity, or sexual orientation, you can also contact The American Civil Liberties Union or one of various group-oriented civil-right groups like the NAACP, JDL, ADL, Americans with Disabilities or

The Fine Art Of Getting Even

ACTU-UP, or similar groups where ever you happen to be.

Well that pretty much covers the Internet.

Remember Grasshopper, if you are not really savy about working with computers, you would be well advised not to attempt a revenge campaign using the World Wide Web.

The FBI, NSA, and most of the local Police Departments have very good people working for them. I know because I have done some consulting myself with a few of these agencies. Although it is not quite like the T.V. shows "NCIS" or "CSI / Cyper" you can be traced. If they can get your IP address most of the time they can get your physical address and then it is all over but the crying.

With that note we will move on to other ways to cause your Mark distress and upset. With any luck he or she may get an ulcer or end up with high blood pressure.

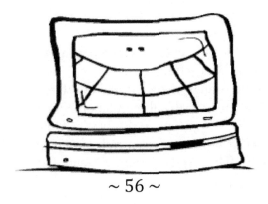

Chapter 9 / Destructive Revenge

Some cautionary notes

Destructive payback has both its advantages and disadvantages.

One thing in particular that you should consider is the fact that many people have their property insured, and although you may momentarily put the Mark into agony, the real cost are often carried by the innocent insurance companies if such a creature actually exists. There might be a fixed price that the owner must cover before the insurance company starts paying any damage. You better check this out in any case.

Another problem with destructive payback is that you will be moving a lot closer to the Mark and/or his property. This will automatically put you in jeopardy of being exposed, and this is particularly bad as you could well find yourself in conflict with the law.

This is why these schemes are the ones that should be most carefully planned before being carried out. It is important that these plans include the daily routine of your Mark, even though he might break this routine at any time.

When you have his routine you also have a better knowledge on how and when to hit him.

A backup plan is certainly not the last thing you should think of here, as you should know what to do if and when you are detected.

Chapter 10 / The Mark's car

If it weren't for car alarms and locked garages, cars would be the easiest of all targets. It still might be that your Mark has his car in his driveway, just locked, but still pretty much accessible.

Your research should already have given you ideas on how accessible your Mark's car is. Even though his car has a car alarm, there are still a few schemes available for you to implement.

Such as, the "old cat nip trick" if the Mark has a convertible. First you go to the pet store and buy a bunch of cat nip. Then you take it home and steep a strong batch of "Catnip Tea". You will also need a squirt gun or spray bottle. Put the Catnip Tea in the squirt gun or spray bottle and under the cover of darkness spray down his or her convertible top with the solution. The neighborhood cats will love you! There are plenty of ways to ruin a car without using the old non-creative "slice-a-car-tire" scheme.

Specialized paint jobs

Get some spray paint and spray-paint some text onto the side of his car. A friend of mine told me this was used during the mid-seventies by a feminist group somewhere in Europe when they went along and sprayed "whore customer!" on the side of whore-customer's cars. Other things that could be written includes, "DRUG DEALER!", "I cheated on my wife", "Registered sex offender", "Paroled rapist", "Child molester" or simply "I love to kill cats!"

Customized paint jobs.

A white car easily turns into a Dalmatian dog look-a-like by spraying black dots onto it. Cut a circle in a piece of cardboard if you want to do a neat job. Other symbols might also be appropriate, depending on who your Mark is, like Nazi-symbols, inverted crosses, Satanic symbols, or just anything that would really scare your Mark.

Paint stripper.

At an auto supply store you can get a can of paint stripper.
Gloves are recommended as this stripper is strongly acidic. It only takes a couple of seconds to walk by a car with this. Silicone sprayed onto cars also does wonders with the paint. You might even check something called liquid scratch.
These schemes work great if the car is parked outside your Mark's apartment, and you only need the guts to do a little walk-by.

Bologna.

Bologna is said to have the most astonishing effect on car paint. Just place some slices on the hood of the car when it is a bit dewy outside and

let it dry in with the morning sun the next day.

The cheaper the Bologna the better. The result is Polka-dot paint!

Attachments.

Small plastic lizard or other cute little kid toys make nice hood ornaments.

Apply superglue of any sort and place them at the front of the hood where some cars have their company shield.

You can also buy a corrosive or an oxidizing agent from your local hardware store; pour it on your Mark's exhaust or anywhere else where it would have an effect.

At the windshield

Next is the windshield, which you can totally ruin by getting one of those glue sticks that is used in hot glue guns. Warm the stick in your hand a little and smear it out onto your Mark's windshield.

You can also use concrete sealant which is a nasty, sticky liquid used to water seal concrete after it is poured. When you've spread it on the windshield it will appear like a lovely cloudy, yellow coating.

Wipers.

A different way to ruin a windshield is to first put some glue onto the windshield wipers, and then add some sand onto the glue.

The Fine Art Of Getting Even

Just make sure the wipers don't get close to the windshield before the glue has dried. Next time your Mark is using the wipers, he'll scratch up his own windshield.

Other substances that do nicely on your Mark's windshield include corn oil, vaseline, tar or paint. If you want to be subtle about it, you can pour it into an open plastic bag and just throw it onto the windshield. Or if you are able to get under the hood put it in the windshield washer fluid container and let him or her do it to themselves.

The heater intake vent.

When you're done playing with the windshield, pour a couple of eggs down the heater intake vent on the car. Wipe off anything that doesn't go in the vent so the Mark doesn't know it's in there. They may notice a strange smell at first, but nothing compared to how it will smell in a few days.

If you are out of eggs, try fox urine lure from your local hunting supply store. You can use a syringe to retrieve and deploy the fox urine from the original bottle. This way you can save yourself from the foul stench and at the same time it will make it easier to spray the urine onto the rubber gaskets or the coating that seals the windows and doors.

Other substances that fit nicely into the vent are milk, urine, strong acids or liquid rust. You can also make your own cocktail by putting some shrimp-shells into a bottle of water, then let it rest in the sun for a week or two, or you could take a potato, slice a deep cut in it and scrub it with dirt. Put it into an airtight

The Fine Art Of Getting Even

container filled with water and close it. Bacteria from the mud will consume the potato, creating a foul stench, granted there's no access to air.

Raising tire havoc

An easy way to fix the tires is to remove or add the balancing weights from the wheels. The tires will be out of balance and driving will not be good for either the tires or the suspension.
The Mark will have to spend some time and money on having a garage rebalance the tires.
This next one requires some work, but if you get some trusted friends (again remember trust is a fleeting love, give it away carefully)with you, then you can put your Mark's car on blocks and take off all the nuts on the wheels. Put super-glue on the threads of the bolts and screw on the nuts as tightly as possible. File the edges of the nuts so a wrench cannot easily grip them. Puncture all four tires. His mechanic will need literally weeks to get it back on the road. Red Loctite is better when used on fasteners. Heat up the lug-nuts until they're red hot. This will surely play havoc on aluminum rims and possibly warp brake rotors.

Under the hood fun and games

The engine is usually the least accessible part of your Mark's car.

The Fine Art Of Getting Even

Still there are lots of things you can do if you're lucky enough to get into it, or under it. For instance, get two or three cans of shaving foam. Open the hood of your Mark's car and set them on the exhaust manifold (that place will be hot). You may need some duct tape to keep them in place. When the engine warms up, the cans explode, covering the engine with shaving foam. If you use WD40 (oil) or deodorant, then the can will explode and the car might catch fire.

This is not recommended as it might injure your Mark or even innocent bystanders.

Under the hood there is tons of stuff to do. If you come prepared (as you should), you can drop a bolt (about 3/4 inch) into the sparkplug holes, and the cylinders will fracture and total the engine.

At a hardware store you can buy a small can of butane, the kind you use to refill a lighter. Drill a small hole in your Mark's distributor cap. Squirt a small amount of butane in and quickly cover the hole with duct tape. When the car starts up, the sparking in the distributor will set off the butane, blowing the distributor cap right off the engine.

Stealing the distributor will prevent your Mark from starting the car.

The Fine Art Of Getting Even

Take the distributor cap out and run a graphite pencil over the rotor blades / brushes, this will make the engine sputter and misfire.

There's a solution available from Force Ten that can turn oil into Jello.

You can also introduce Styrofoam, naphtha or tide into the engine oil. Or get a can of valve grinding powder and put it in the oil.

The easiest way is to get under the car, with a container and a wrench, then open the oil-screw beneath the car and let the oil run into the container. Tighten the screw and get yourself out of the area. Or just loosen the bolt so it will fall out as the Mark drives.

Often the oil-warning lamp will malfunction and the engine will be totally inoperable.

Anti-freeze added to the oil turns it into a brown, milky foam. Even if no direct damage is done, the Mark and/or his/her mechanic will think there is a blown head gasket or a cracked head or block, leading to very expensive repairs.

Moving on into the battery compartment and put three or four Alka-Seltzers into it or some other substance like oil or soap.

Next, slide in under the front of the car, and poke a hole in the lower radiator hose by using a sharp ice pick. The puncture would close itself and everything would be just fine until the engine gets up to a critical temperature and then the coolant will blow out the hole.

While you are under there take out two of the four 3/8 or 1/2 inch bolts that hold the drive shaft universal joint to the transmission and loosen the other two. It

The Fine Art Of Getting Even

may not happen right away but I guarantee the Mark will have an interesting ride one day.

The Mark's gas tank

The gas tank is also a popular place to stuff things into. The most common being sugar, but ping-pong balls slit halfway through, filled with crystal Drano also does the job. Use a balloon with a tiny hole or something similar, when you live in the states where the hole ain't big enough for ping pong balls.

Crystal Drano is a chemical used to unclog pipes. Tape the ping-pong ball together again after applying the Drano. The ping-pong ball will dissolve in the gasoline, and when the Drano gets in touch with the fuel a violent chemical reaction will occur. Rumor has it that it'll even stand a van on it's nose. My suggestion is that you leave this at the thought.

Other things to put into the fuel tank could be crushed cork, silicone carbide or icing sugar.

Dissolve some mothballs in gas and add it to your Mark's tank. This will make the engine run hot. The engine oil breaks down, and then the engine seizes. It is hard to trace and damage is already done when the person realizes the engine is hot.

Sabotaging the fuel line could be done by making a hole in the fuel tank.

Afterwards you may call the fire department and they'll come tow the car away and give the owner a stiff fine.

The Fine Art Of Getting Even

Some other car action

One way of getting back at your Mark is to tie his car to something on his house. A front balcony might be just fine, or attach it to the doorknob on a gardening house door. Use a solid rope or a chain, about twenty or thirty yards is more than enough. Cover it with sand or something. The longer the rope is, the more speed he will have gained before anything happens.

You can have a lot of fun with bumper stickers. Get some sort of racially offensive bumper sticker and put them onto his car.

Survey the local area and find out what ethnic group is the most militant, and use something that goes against that group in your scheme. Otherwise, use generic "White/Black Power", or whatever. If the car is parked next to a handicapped space, some pushing might be all that is needed to move it into the handicapped space. Put an antipolice bumper sticker on its bumper and call the police. You could enhance this by putting a little bag of pot past the doorframe where it can be seen. Or, just removing the yearly sticker from his tag. Police just love to respond to drivers that fail to renew their tags. This works well in apartment complexes that have tow away services checking their resident's cars.

Best to do it when you know the Mark has gone away for a few days. That way he does not get to see the notice on the car before the towing service tows it

The Fine Art Of Getting Even

away. It will cost him for the towing and the storage of the car plus a new sticker for the tag.

At times your Mark might be a neighbor who has a cheap car alarm that constantly goes off. This is a problem that might be solved easily. I recommend you write a nice message on a piece of paper, wrap it around a brick and place the brick on top of the hood of the offending car whose alarm constantly goes off. The message should say something like, "Next time your alarm goes off, this brick will go through your window - prick." This is more a solution than a severe revenge scheme.

Other schemes might include totally saran wrapping the Mark's car (coat it with blank plastic used to pack food), tucking it into bandaids, or do like some students in a Midwestern state who got their hands on a large amount of plaster bandages, the kind wrapped around splints which harden and form a cast. It took four of them ten minutes to completely mummify the car, and then they ran a hose over it and hardened it solid.

On cold nights you may put a lawn sprinkler on the top of your Mark's car. Let the sprinkler run with just a little bit of water through all the night. By morning there should be a thick layer of ice coating the whole car.

Another dirty trick is to just go and squirt a small tube of superglue into each of the door locks. The best time to do this is if the Mark is at a restaurant or bar late at night on a weekend. The locksmith will just love to come out on overtime and after hours pay to get the sap into his or her car.

Chapter 11 / The residence

The Mark's home is his personal ground. It is close to him, the place where he usually should feel safe and private. Violating this ground is often difficult, yet rewarding at the same time.

Security and surveillance should be paid much attention in these cases. You don't have to be technical about it actually it might be as easy as sneaking into a party which your Mark is having. You could also get yourself some lock-picking equipment (and experience) but then we would be talking about breaking in, and last time I checked it was a still illegal to do so. Dorm rooms are more easily accessible, but you would still be breaking in. There are pages on the Internet that talk about lock picking one well known originating from MIT is easily obtainable on the Internet.

Dorms and similar places

College dorms have all one thing in common, shoddy workmanship.

Due to the design of the doors, it is possible to wedge a number of pennies between the doorframe and the door when the door is locked. Push the door as far in as you can while it is locked, then wedge pennies between the frame and the catch. This is known as "pennying" a door. It might be that someone has already played this on you, and if you want to escape through such a trap, simply pull the door towards you as hard as you can, kick the door in the corner below the catch. This should dislodge the pennies.

Dorm doors are also easy targets for signs saying, "Do not disturb! Masturbating intensely!" They should be as easy to make as tearing them down. The more you go hanging them up after your Mark has torn them down, the more annoying they get. You could also apply the old, glass-n-glue trick to this one. Take a bucket of wallpaper glue and thoroughly crush some glass into it. Put some glue onto the door, hang up the poster, and then put glue onto the poster. This trick was widely used by political left-wingers in the seventies when their posters often were torn down by their opponents. If you want to make certain that nobody gets permanent injuries, I suggest you leave the glass out.

One prankish way of getting back at your Mark in a dorm, is to get a few hundred plastic cups. When the

The Fine Art Of Getting Even

Mark is away for the weekend, or the whole day, pick his door lock and get into his room. Fill the cups with water and place them one-by-one to cover the entire floor in his room. I suggest you find some friends to help you with this one.

One different prank that has been played at several dorms in the country, where co-students had covered the dorm door with a brick wall (making the room disappear) while the Mark was on a weekend holiday. You can probably find references and pictures of this on the net.

Doors in general

Doors are nice targets for substances that have a foul stench.

Scramble some eggs. Add some green food dye and a little bit of garlic salt. Pour it all over your Mark's door or doormat. Let it soak in for a good while, while your Mark is away for the weekend. Other things that you can smear onto doors are animal defecation, tar, chlorine or something foul smelling mentioned earlier in the car section of this book.

Any garden hose carrying water is a nice tool for the ones seeking to get even. Hook up the hose, push it through the mail-slot on the front door and then simply turn it on. A funny variation here is to use your Mark's neighbor's garden hose. You should also spray some kind of sealer at the bottom of the door to make the house hold more water.

If you use a good window insulator, you might even be able to seal the whole door shut. Check around your local hardware store to find the best suitable insulator.

Television terrorism

Let's say that your Mark is living in an area where they have cable TV. On the outside you will find one of the boxes they use to connect the main wire to the different houses. Open the box, unhook wires, flip switches and do whatever seems good. Close the box and get to a pay phone, call and tell the cable company that you saw your Mark messing around with the box. This works great if your Mark doesn't have cable. You could also drag a wire from the box to his house. Another thing you can do is to find where the cable is buried. Dig it up, cut it and use some black tape to cover the cutting. The Cable Company will most likely need a few days to find the error. Use this tactic during the Olympics or any other big event. If your Mark is the Cable Company then do this at several places. You can also short circuit the cable by putting a metal piece into in, e.g. use a needle or anything similar to connect the ground to the main signal.

Loud music

Quite a few people have experienced situations where their next door apartment neighbor is playing loud music at night, and where reasoning with him doesn't help. It might be frustrating, but there are ways to fight this kind of neighbor. Get a cheap plug-in radio and a large cardboard box. Open one end of the box, put the radio in and tape the open end firmly against the wall next to their bedroom. Keep the box off the floor, no reason to disturb the ones downstairs. Tune the radio to a station with any music that your Mark doesn't like. The radio doesn't have to be very loud the box acts as an acoustic coupler to the wall. The bigger the box the better. Turn the radio on when you get up. Off when you go to sleep.

Do this every day. If anybody asks why just say you're afraid of burglars. When the asshole next door stops by to complain, use the same arguments that he used when you complained to him about loud music. A different approach to the same problem could be to just get yourself a large bowling ball. Hold it up in the air and drop down on the floor. Do this at random intervals throughout the day. This naturally only works if it is the neighbor's downstairs who causes you trouble. A variation of this is to get a big weightlifting plate. Put the plate on the floor and spin it around like you would with a quarter on a tabletop. Jump on the weight when it's just about to settle.

The bathroom

Now let's move into the bathroom. These schemes would be executed at a party or at a public toilet. Saran wrap is fun. You can also wrap it over the top of the toilet bowl on your Mark's toilet and then put the seat down. This works especially well if your Mark is a woman. Pour syrup on the toilet seat. You can't readily see it, but your Mark will stick to the seat. Some toilets have black toilet seats.

Tar works nicely on these. At night, or at least at a time when you suspect nobody would use the toilet for a few hours, pour a large amount of Jello powder into the bowl or the tank. Cement mix also works nicely. Also, the ketchup packets you get at junk food restaurants can be placed between the lid and the bowl. Make sure to make a tiny hole in the packet first. Now when your Mark sits down, he will get a red surprise all over the backs of his knees.

While you are in the bathroom, and in the close reach of your Mark's shower: Take a pill capsule, preferably one made of gelatin. Open it and fill with methylene blue, which comes in powder-form used mainly for dye, and can be bought in drug stores or aquarium-related stores (as it is used as a remedy for some fish diseases.) It is nontoxic but still very good at making stains. Fill the capsule with the powder. Smear the capsule in with some Vaseline. Insert it into showerhead. When the Mark uses the shower, the blue dye will leak out and stain him.

You can also put a bouillon cube or two into the showerhead. With the hot water, the bouillon cube will melt and the Mark will probably not notice until it is too late. If you are out of bouillon, use Kool-Aid, preferably the violet grape one, as it makes really good stains.

Nair or any other hair removal is a nasty replacement for shampoo.

Applying Nair to a shampoo bottle might appear a bit complex. The problem is that Nair has a distinct smell and if you use too much of it, the Mark will notice. One way of fighting this is to pour some of the shampoo into a cup. Add a little Nair at a time until you can smell it in the shampoo bottle, then add a little bit of shampoo. The result may vary from your Mark losing all his hair to him losing just big chunks of his hair. If you suspect that the Mark will have the shampoo in the hair for just too short of a time, then put Nair into the conditioner instead.

The bedroom

After the bathroom, get into the kitchen and pick up some sugar. Use this sugar afterwards in your Mark's bedroom. Just spread it out on his bed, under his bed sheets. A thin layer of plastic between the bed sheets and the bed would cause the body to heat up the sugar which you would put on the plastic. When your Mark wakes up he'll look and feel like a glazed donut. Replace the sugar with milk powder to get unbelievable results. When the milk powder gets into the pores, it stays there and turns sour. Your Mark will smell of sour milk for almost a week. Chocolate bars in the bed sheets can also be a pain, even though it is more obvious and easier to detect before any damage is done.

The Fine Art Of Getting Even

One scheme that works well in military
quarters is to wait until your Mark is on
leave. Then sneak into his room and sew
alfalfa into his bed. Add a little bit of water
and in a week or so it will grow up and make
a nice bed when your Mark returns.

The garden

Under the cover of a dark night, you could easily get
an opportunity to sneak into your Mark's garden, do
some damage and then get out without getting caught.
During the day you would do better by not sneaking
in, as it would look strange. Instead you should
pretend to be a gardener, a pool caretaker, a cable guy
or even someone from the electric company.
Dressing up in stealthy clothing usually brings more
attention than wanted. Dress casual, avoid sharp
colors and you should be fine.

The lawn

Salt works great for killing lawns permanently. Use a
relatively large quantity of sea-salt and spread it
around the whole lawn. Similar effects can be
achieved by using lime, weed seeds or even diesel
fuel. For the artistic avenger I recommend writing
anything from "bitch!" to "Asshole!" Any simple
word would do as long sentences and words are
harder to read. Also, unless you're doing this at night,
you should not set the fuel on fire as it will make the
grass die, where applied, and have the wanted effect
in less time.

The Fine Art Of Getting Even

The opposite effect is achieved by spreading fertilizer onto the lawn. It will cause the grass to grow twice as fast on the places where you've spread it. If you use too much fertilizer, then the grass will change color.

Frosted flakes also look nice on a lawn. Go to the Mark's house late at night and spread the flakes out all over their lawn. The morning dew will moisten the flakes slightly; then, the sun comes out and bakes them into one huge frosted flake. Later, when the ants come, it could get really entertaining.

Seagulls love bread, and one awesome way to feed them is to throw bits of old bread into your Mark's garden at night. At dawn the birds will discover the food and they will have a little party on the Mark's lawn. The great thing about birds is that they just can't shut up while partying, so they will most likely wake your Mark up in the midst of their feast, and they'll not leave easily either.

It is not a nice thing to do, but there have been some cases where people have extended the previous scheme by adding alcohol to the bread. You can probably imagine for yourself what effect that might have on the poor birds, especially if someone should call the police from a phone booth, claiming that they saw the Mark feed the seagulls with poisoned bread.

Plastic forks are great. You can get huge quantities of them for a low price, and with fellow avengers you can plant them into your Mark's garden at night, preferably when he's on a vacation. This scheme might be mild, but fun to implement and gives quite an annoyance for the Mark.

The Fine Art Of Getting Even

Trees

Destroying a tree is easy. Make a salt solution by adding water to salt, stir and then pour it at the base of the tree. Another way, one more obvious, is to strip about six inches of bark round the tree. This will prevent the nutrients produced by the leaves to get to the roots for storage and vice versa. You can also ruin your Mark's tree by applying copper tacks or nails. Put them into the roots and clip off their heads, and they'll be as good as invisible. One method that I learned from the environmentalist (it was also

featured in an X-files episode) was to put huge steel nails into the tree. When the Mark, in this case a timbering company, came to cut it down, they got their equipment ruined by the heavy-duty nail. You should think carefully before implementing this scheme as the chainsaw chain could snap and seriously injure the logger, and you don't want to hurt an innocent person.

The garage

Your Mark might not have such a big garden, but it could be that he owns a garage. There are limits to what you can do with locked garage, but painting stuff, like large dots, on the side of the garage is really something to consider. Your Mark will have to spend both time and money removing it. Inside his garage there are certainly several things that could be done, but this depends a bit on who your Mark is and what he has inside his garage. Putting nails, the sharp ones with big flat backs which are often used to hang up posters, onto the garage floor is usually a good start.

The mailbox

Another annoying scheme can be as simple as putting rocks into your Mark's mailbox each morning. This could be done before your Mark goes off to work, or when he has left. Just remember what was said earlier about tampering with mail and mailboxes, which in most cases are considered federal offences. For the more advanced avenger I suggest building a pyramid of rocks on your Mark's lawn.

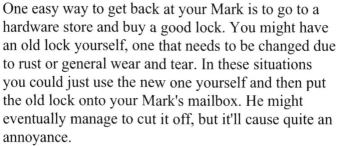

Most things can be thrown into your Mark's lawn, things like garbage, cod, pasta, paint, paper, eggs, defecation, images of Mao, rocks, porn magazines, tomb stones and your Mark's neighbor's things are all popular.

One easy way to get back at your Mark is to go to a hardware store and buy a good lock. You might have an old lock yourself, one that needs to be changed due to rust or general wear and tear. In these situations you could just use the new one yourself and then put the old lock onto your Mark's mailbox. He might eventually manage to cut it off, but it'll cause quite an annoyance.

Ants and other insects love honey. Pour some honey into his mailbox, or fill the whole mailbox with cement. Also if the mailbox has a flag, you can glue it upwards using superglue.

Walls, fountains and bugs

Concrete walls make good arenas for walls. Don't just tag the wall with random profanities; be artistic about it as that will give it more attention. There is a special kind of graffiti that really sticks around.
Get a big sheet of paper and write your message on it with liquid Ajax or Comet. Take the paper where the wall is, douse it in lighter fluid, stick it to the wall, make a lighter fluid trail away from the wall and light it. The whole thing burns in about one second, so there is no fire danger (unless you applied it to a material that easily burn), but your message gets stuck to the wall by a chemical process, and it is almost impossible to get it off without painting over it.
Crickets could become nice pets for your Mark. They are cheap, noisy and usually available at your local pet-shop or bait shop. Release them in the evening, or at night through your Mark's window or into the mail slot. This is something you should time to be done the night before his exam, or some other big event. Do not do this if your Mark lives in your neighborhood, as these critters move around.
For the Mark with a fountain I recommend getting some coloring dye, or if you wish to be more advanced; Kodak and other chemical companies sell certain classes of chemicals called surfactants.

These essentially make water more slippery. In a fountain with low tolerance, water hits 1 inch from the edge. A good surfactant can send the water splashing 3 inches beyond the fountain pool. This drains the fountain in short order, and burns out the pump. There are certainly many other things that which you can apply to the pool like oil, bubble bath, soap, cement, colored dye, dead animals, defecation, moth balls, dead or live fish, stuff bought at Taco Bell, etc.

The kitchen

The kitchen is the last place on this tour. This is a place where you could really go bonkers, because there are so many small items around in this room. Mix the different spices or just swap salt and sugar. Do the same with corn, wheat, oatmeal, or whatever he's got.

Pour the milk out and replace it with water. Move round the different kitchen appliances. Put a Snickers bar into his microwave oven and let it run for a while. This will generate a foul stench, and it looks nasty too.

Put grease on the top of the stove, if it is electric. There are things you can do to a gas-stove that I should probably not mention here.

Let's just leave this to the movies and our fantasy, exploding gas is no fun.

Grease and soya oil is a pain to wash away. Exploit this by pouring it around randomly. Top it by spreading whatever combinations of wheat, flour, oatmeal, corn, baking soda and spice you can find, onto the floor.

Chapter 12 / The work place

Introduction

From working at quite a few places I have found that one can always divide the workforce into three groups. The friendly, the hostile, and the hostile who have some kind of leadership position. The first group would be your random work buddy which in most cases would be almost all of the work force. You don't want to mess with your buddies too much or they'll perceive you as being one of the idiots in the hostile group. Still a few shenanigans among friends are common and in most cases bonding. Just make sure you don't pick on the same friendly target each time. I will only cover this briefly here as this book is not about pranks.

Friends and foes

The strange thing about these two groups is that they often seem to collaborate. The hostile in a leader position would actually find it very handy to have some kind of informant in the group of "common" workers. Slander and mischief expressed in this group would then get back to him and he would know exactly who to fire or watch out for. The traitor would benefit from this by being the first in line when the word promotion is mentioned.

The Fine Art Of Getting Even

One thing you should be aware of is that there is always a leader who is above your leader, either a major CEO, a senator or congressman or even the customers of the business.

The friendly

An old trick that has provided prankster's hours of entertainment is to wait for your Mark to take a little coffee break. When your Mark is away, grab his telephone and tape down (using clear scotch tape) the button where the receiver sits. When your Mark returns, give him a little call and watch the confusion. A variation of this one is to place small pieces of tape over the holes to the speaker.

Create a stupid rule or regulation. If possible, make it seem like a rule that would be under your Mark's area of responsibility. Print it on the company printer, and hang it up on a display board. Write your Mark's name at the bottom of the note and start complaining (to everyone but him). One similar idea involves putting up a police wanted poster with your Mark's name and picture on it.

Sending messages from one employer to another is another wonderful prank. This could also be considered severe, but if you hide your tracks you need not worry.

The hostile

You might want be careful with the hostile co-worker. This is typically the Mark who goes behind

The Fine Art Of Getting Even

your back, making quite an effort to bring you trouble. Whatever you do, go undetected and untraceable, because if these individuals find out that you're somehow on to them they'll increase their effort and make your working day even more like a living hell.

At the office

Copy-machines can be useful tools for your revenge purpose, the same goes for FAX machines. Invent something that looks conspicuous, put the paper into the photocopier and leave it there. Others will find it, wonder what it is and have a look at it. Finally they find your Marks name on it and maybe

confront him with it. Naturally he'll deny it and make everything look even more conspicuous.

Themes that could be applied here are industrial espionage, or even a scheme for a new system to monitor the work-force, supposed to be hidden or at least not something that would be detected by your co-workers.

Another popular scheme involves having a florist deliver flowers to your Mark. Take a look in the yellow pages and find a florist who delivers singing telegrams or a theatrical delivery. The kicker here is to have the flowers sent from someone of the opposite gender of your Mark's attraction. You can also play two Marks up against each other on this.

This scheme could be brought a bit further. Search your yellow pages or ads in newspapers for adult or escort services. Call them up and leave the phone number and Mark's name in the voice-mail or on their beepers. This works best if someone else is likely to answer your Mark's phone.

Chapter 13 / The computer

Any computers that aren't behind locked doors or secured with a password are easy targets for the computer literate avenger. The great thing about computers is that you can do anything from prankish stuff like changing the color configuration of your Mark's PC to really ruining months or even years of work by killing the hard disk.

Messing with software

At the work place, one nice scheme involves installing graphic images in the background on your Mark's workstation. This is as easy as  changing the colors. Either have the image ready in JPEG format on a diskette or download it anonymously from a location on the Internet.
One variation of this one involves manipulating images of a second Mark employee (by scanning the picture and merging it with another picture from the said location on the Internet.) This could lead to an interesting discussion between the two Marks. Photo Shop is the way to go with this.
Altering the desktop configuration is also easy. I have already mentioned changing colors, but you should not stop there. For instance, remove all the icons from the desktop (and the menus) and change the screen

format to the lowest possible resolution with a minimum of colors. This is truly annoying and at worst it will take your Mark an hour to fix everything.

Getting serious

As the crime gets more severe, so should the punishment. Consider an scumbag that has been working on a project for months and has all his work on his PC.

Your Mark could be anything from a corporate office worker to a student. As long as he doesn't have a backup of his work, he is going to get screwed. And sadly for them most people do not back up their work  There are certainly different ways to kill data, one being just to erase them by typing erase/delete or using some kind of directory browser.

In UNIX-like operating systems one can erase whole directories by using the "rm -rf (dir)"command. One problem that you still will face is the fact that some operating systems don't delete the whole file, but rather the internal entry saying where the file is located and the name of it, or parts of that information. This means that the data can still be restored with special undelete programs. And expensive recovery technicians.

To make it harder for your Mark to restore data, you could make yourself a boot-disk that contains the program fdisk and format. The boot disk that

Windows 98 supplies is sufficient for this purpose. Use fdisk to delete and recreate the whole hard-disk, and then use format to physically delete the data afterwards. You can also low-level format the disk, if it is a SCSI disk.

Viral plagues

Viruses are considered to be quite a menace and I wouldn't advise using one even if you know what you are doing. There are many virus-sites on the net, and some of them have live viruses. Download at your own risk. There are also programs around that do not replicate themselves and do less damage; these are mostly just annoying and therefore suitable for the more mild revenge schemes.

The BIOS

Another easy way to mess up a computer is to play around in the computer BIOS. The BIOS menus are accessed at startup time, when the computer runs checks on the RAM and the disks. Usually you get a message on the screen saying that you can hit DEL for the BIOS setup menu. Do this and start playing around. If the computer has an unset BIOS password, set it and the Mark will have to open the computer casing and reset the BIOS completely.

Messing with hardware

Avengers who don't want to mess around with the
software could still do a lot of damage to the
hardware.
Open the computer, usually by just using a
screwdriver, and have a look at the inventory. You
will find that there are banks of RAM, cables,
motherboard, drives and one or more CPUs. If you
take a look at the CPU you will find that it usually has
a heat-sink attached to it. Remove it, and the CPU
will get hot and eventually it
will malfunction or it might
even get cooked with
permanent damage.
Removing one or more
RAM banks could be useful,
but you should leave at least
one or the computer will not
start, unless that was your
idea in the first place.

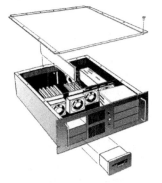

The subtle revenge seeker

More subtle avenger would simply put a screwdriver
into the fan, causing it to deform and make a lot of
noise while in operation. At worst it could
malfunction causing heat to build up in the computer.
Removing the CPU fan is even better, but you would
have to open the casing to do this.

The berserker

When everything above seems like too much trouble, use a hammer randomly inside the casing will definitely do permanent damage. If even that is too much trouble, grab the whole PC, after disconnecting all the cables, and drop it off in a nearby garbage container.

Chapter 14 / The institutional

Institutions such as the government, the police, companies, schools or the military are often acting in a way that makes them justifiable Marks. The arrogance occasionally displayed by individuals in these institutions sometimes reflects only their apparent status as being untouchable.

This is backed up with the enormous resources that the institution has. It is becoming more and more rare these days that the average man in the street wins court cases against either the government or the police, even in cases where the guilt of the institution is proven and documented beyond doubt.

With that being said I want to state that revenge against an institution is a very difficult endeavor and should be thought about long and hard prior to enactment.

The government I am going to use the governmental context for a wide variety of services here. Revenge against the government is rarely a successful endeavor. And will lead to you finding yourself in deep do-do real quick. Avoid these attacks at all cost. They just are not worth the trouble!

The Fine Art Of Getting Even

The police

The police are sometimes targeted for unjustified revenge. This, because the public often feel badly treated when they get tickets for illegal parking, speeding or similar petty incidents. The fact is that the police have an obligation to follow and can't be blamed for following the rules (laws) set by politicians or lawmakers. If the law is what you have a problem with, target the politician and make your protests out loud.

I really do not recommend doing anything on location as far as revenge against the police goes. History shows than the best way to tangle your way out of these situations is to play along and either accept or reject the fine, depending on the situation you are in. Accepting it even if you did nothing wrong might seem idiotic, but if the fine is low, you would have to ask yourself is it worth the trouble of going through a trial or not. In any case if you broke the law, you should accept the fine and forget about revenge. You would naturally get the name of the officers and perform some long distance revenge scheme, if you decided to act upon the wronged action. It is a lot easier if your wrath is aimed directly towards the police station itself.

Got a parking ticket?

It might happen that you get a parking ticket you don't deserve. What one does in these situations is maybe manufacture your own replica using a PC and a good printer. Spend a couple of evenings wandering the streets and place the fake parking bills onto random cars, which naturally are legally parked. You achieve two things by doing this. One, you get quite a few people to complain about the bill. Two, you get a few suckers who actually pay the bill. How the police or the parking department handles this depends, but they do not have anything outstanding on these people so they have to return the money, costing work time and unnecessary administration.

Another way of causing harm to the ones handling parking is very simple, just put a plastic bag over the parking meter. People probably will still park there, without paying. For private parking companies this will work well, as it will lower their income.

For those cases when you have two Marks, one being the police/ parking authorities and the other is a sucker with a parked car: Call the towing company and have his car towed claiming that he was parking in your slot.

Politicians

Politicians often seem like distant revenge targets, but you should remember that these too are people who have cars, gardens, homes, phones, etc. Often there are a lot of people around them, which complicates things but doesn't make a neat revenge scheme impossible.

The Fine Art Of Getting Even

Scandals are one way of getting back at a politician, but as we have often seen, the politicians often have ways of crawling themselves out of any situation. And indeed, who is the public to trust when they see one unknown girl claiming to have a relationship with the leader of a nation, while the leader himself is saying it never took place?

Still, scandals could be effective, especially if you know how to play the media.

Otherwise it is quite easy to hit the politician directly using any of the other tactics described in this book. One rather mild one is to forge letters from the politician to the media or a secondary Mark.

Hospitals

Hospitals may seem like apparently easy targets, but do keep in mind that you might hurt or even kill innocent people who relies on the services provided. Bringing down the particular person who has wronged you, a Doctor for instance, is better. One way of doing that is to spread news among the drug addicts in your community that this doctor prescribes drugs, for a little extra fee, with no questions asked. You would naturally be a part of that environment to make it sound right, or in a smaller community you could get the right effect by telling your friend about it. Rumors in small communities are an incredible tool and will serve your efforts well, no matter who your Mark is.

The Fine Art Of Getting Even

Tax collectors are your friends

Another great tool for revenge business is the IRS (Tax collectors.)
You would need the Mark's social security number and as much information about your Mark as possible. Contact your local IRS field office. Using the Mark's name and information, advise them that you have been filing false returns for years, not declaring money (from illegal gambling, drug dealing, etc. make it sound believable) advise them that you have turned over a new leaf and want to make amends. Set up an appointment with the IRS agent to set things right. When the Mark doesn't show up for his appointment, for obvious reasons, the IRS will send a field agent to the Mark's address.

Odds are the Mark will be audited no matter what. Another, more direct method involves forging a tax form using the name and information on your Mark. In the US you can get the 1040-EZ or 1040-A package. Type the name, address, city, state, zip, SS and filing status normally. Prepare the rest of the return with anti-tax and anti-government statements typed in strategic places on the form. In other words use your own discretion.

Prepare the official return envelope in the same manner.

A different approach to this last one is to fill out a form with information of a high income. Use the yellow pages and get some addresses of companies who are rumored to do a lot of unreported (tax-wise)

work. This is a perfect scheme for the scumbag who doesn't care about delivering any tax report form at all.

The Company

One great way to get back at a company, like a pub or a garage, is to put an advertisement into the local newspaper where it says that they're selling one of their products at a ridiculously low price. For a garage you can write that they're offering free checks on people's cars or $0.99 oil changes. Timing should be accurate. Do this when everyone is looking to buy this service or product.

The bank

There might be a situation where the Mark is a bank that has wrongfully taken money from your account. When that is the case, go to the bank and rent a small safe deposit box. After you've gotten one, bring with you a bag of fish substance that will reek after a couple of days at room temperature. The bank will naturally have your name and number, and they will beg you to remove it. Remind them of the cash that was stolen and try to negotiate with them. Eventually, they can open the box without your permission, but it takes a while, so don't put anything illegal into it.

The good cause

You could also give money in your Mark's business name to every charity, religious group and political action possible. You could either give small amounts of money to groups that your Mark is heavily against, or to groups that you know will come back later and harass him for more money.

Have a company which produces t-shirts at a low price make some for you. Do a bogus logo and his office telephone number, then donate the tee-shirts to a local homeless shelter under his or her name. It would look real funny when people all around start to wear their tee shirts.

Restaurants

The next level of corporate revenge involves junk-food restaurants and drive-through windows.

Wire up a speaker and hide it in the bushes. On the other side you connect an amplifier and a microphone (use your imagination here, anything from a walk-man to a portable computer might come in handy). When someone pulls up to place their order, be as rude as possible while impersonating the clerk. This will hurt the restaurant and it might as well lead to a number of complaints from unsuspecting customers. You could also write a letter to the manager, saying that you were in the drive-through on that particular night and were subjected to this verbal abuse. If this is all too complicated, hang a note saying "out of order" on the set-box.

The Fine Art Of Getting Even

 Flashing can be a crude but effective way of getting even with a restaurant. If you are shy, you can have a friend drive by the restaurant with his ass hanging out the window. I do think the customers would lose their appetite after a slight glimpse of that.

Laundries

Have you ever been ripped off by a laundry store or been in a situation where you've been treated badly by the owner? Go to a washer and fill it up with loads of detergent, soap, grease or paint.
You could also poke holes in the rubber pipes that lead to the washers. Another suggestion is to jam the coin insert part of the machine with dented coins or foreign objects. Add some super-glue and it will take a very long time to fix and result in a lot of lost business and frustrations.

Doctors and dentists

Doctors and dentists always seem to get away with everything, don't they? Well, not anymore. Go to a label printer and have them print a bunch of labels with your Doc's office name and address. Next thing you do is visiting one of those places where you get pornographic magazines. After you've read them, I mean, after you've purchased them, put the label on them and drop them off in the waiting room under the pile of magazines that's already there. Don't wait around unless you have an appointment there.

The Fine Art Of Getting Even

Another thing you can do for doctors is to advertise. Affix street posters with the doctors' name on them in the worst parts of your vicinity. Here you will be helping this doctor selling drug prescriptions with no questions asked.

You could also try to get a job at your Mark's company.

When inside you have a wide range of tactics you can implement and you will be close to anything. Being nasty to customers is a good one, but you could also give them good discounts or do other sabotage. Just don't get caught.

The school

As with the police, teachers are also often targets of wrongful revenge and shenanigans. It doesn't necessarily mean that these teachers are bad teachers, more often it is because the children act like uncivilized savages and feel badly treated when they don't do their homework.

Harassing teachers is not something I condone; actually I don't condone anything in this book, except the copyright notice.

Teachers

Analyzing the teacher could be useful. A fairly old teacher might get an embarrassing problem if you brought your pornographic comics to school. Creative minds could certainly make their own version of, "Peter Penis, Master Detective and the Case of the

The Fine Art Of Getting Even

Missing Coke Bottles." You could also hide things like a condom or a dildo in his drawer.

The idea of putting display board tacks on the teacher's chair is old and quite outdated.

Another way of making the workday of a teacher miserable, is by rubbing lipstick, tar or paint on the doors to the school's administrative offices and the teacher's rest room. Done cleverly it might not be noticed until every teacher is dirty.

In the one-mean-pupil section we have copying off your teacher's signature on the bottom of a resignation. Leave it in the principal's office. Make something up about him getting a new job, and he can't come personally to discuss it. Time this to a period when the Mark is away from work for some days. This can also work in the opposite direction where you pose as the principal firing the teacher.

Fellow students

Another Mark that might deserve your attention, in the school area, is your fellow student or pupil. Most of what is written under the corporate revenge also applies here. In addition, due to the way school works, there are a few good ones.

Ex-Lax or anything that make your Mark's stomach twitch could easily be applied to his drink. Again timing is essential, as the Mark will be more vulnerable at the day of his final examination, although ruining for life might be excessive, ruining him for the semester might be a better choice.

Quite a few places you can cancel exams without identifying yourself. At the places where they do

~ 101 ~

require an ID, try to get a fake one or steal your Mark's ID.

The Mark's locker is an easy target. Put some glue on a toothpick and insert it into the lock. Hang pornographic images on the front side of the locker. Pour fox urine or some other stinky substance on its top or through its holes. If you are good at picking locks, then plant something in the locker and then use the glue and toothpick trick on the lock. Write something creative on the locker door. When the Mark goes away for a week or two, pour milk on top of it, or use a generous amount of cottage cheese squeezed between two plates.

Tape the plate together and hide it on top of his locker or push it into the locker. It will have a nasty odor when he discovers it.

An easy way to get back at school buddies who use drugs frequently is to get a drug testing kit from a drug store. Send the whole kit to his parents along with a letter from either the school or one of his friends who feels that their son or daughter has a problem.

The school building

In the school-building vandalism section we have ideas like drawing obscenities on pull-down maps or movie screens, or hiding foul smelling things above the ceiling. The latter can be done in some governmental buildings where they have ceilings resting on an iron grid, if not, use the air-duct. Maggots (fly larva) can be bought at several sports stores in areas where they use these as fish bait. Get a

box of them and hide it in a classroom, just before the school closes for the summer. Open the lid slightly to let the flies out and when the pupils return next semester it will be swarming with flies in the room.

Clog the drains by pouring cement into the toilets and the sinks. Also always carry screwdrivers and slowly dismantle everything you can.

Have friends help you. Make a competition where the object is to get most screws out.

With access to a PC you can make false announcements from your school. Use the same format style as they use and distribute them to teacher's mailboxes and put them on display boards. The display boards can also be used against your fellow students.

Get a picture of your Mark and write something nasty under it. Sex adds, I-am-stupid posters, or anything from your own creative mind.

On your country's national day, take down the national flag and put up your own. Have a friend lift you up standing on his back. Tie the rope and cut everything that is below, leaving quite a distance down to the ground.

Sticky stuff

Two of the more flexible items used in revenge schemes are superglue and the insulation used as filler in building walls.

Glue

Superglue is perhaps the most versatile "sticky stuff." Just apply it into any key-lock to give your Mark the agony of his life. Car door locks, car fuel locks, school lockers, apartment and house front door locks, mailbox locks or even garage door locks, the variations are endless.

Gluing ornaments like plastic toys to the car hood was already mentioned. This can also be applied to other things, like windows, doors, office desks where pens glued to the desk works great. Your imagination is the limit.

Insulation

Housing insulation also has many applications. These usually come in large spray containers and when applied appear as an expanding foam. The real kicker here is that it soon hardens. One problem here is that when applied to a limited area, the foam will put pressure on its walls, this could also be part of the revenge. Places to apply this are mailboxes, through open windows, into cars, through mail-slots, desk drawers, lockers and onto lawns or up the exhaust pipe of his car.

The yellow insulation that is used to make air conditioning duct works is particularly useful if you are able to get to your Marks clothing. Simply rub it on the inside of their under shorts or the armpit area of their shirts.

The annoying and irritating

Annoying schemes shouldn't be too severe because they usually would have to be repeated frequently and therefore the risk of detection is high. You also shouldn't apply annoying schemes upon a Mark who is patient as a rock. In such situations the energy you spend on the work would easily be higher than the energy and irritation felt by your Mark.

Annoying roommates

Roommates are close and often easy targets for annoyances. I have observed that acting nervous or jumpy often makes other people nervous. Nervousness is often quite closely connected to annoyances. You could start the afternoon by sitting straight looking at the wall (make sure there is a clock within your view) - every five minutes get up, walk to the window, look out and mumble. This would surely be annoying for the duration. The next day, mention that you wonder what you did around that time the previous day. If others ask, tell them that your roommate has been acting strange lately.
If your roommate has a girlfriend then you should be really nice to her. Give her a little gift every now and then, smile at her often and look at her tits when he can see it.
Comment on her ass to her boyfriend and ask if they're into threesomes. Leave pornographic

magazines around your bed. Also talk about yourself and her when he thinks you're sleeping and he is awake.

Have your alarm clock ring at 5AM each morning. First you let it ring for a little while, and when your roommate complains, get up and go to the bathroom. Take a pee, or whatever, just make a bit of noise, then return to your bed. Do this every morning for a while.

The next tactic involves getting some old keys. This can be done at a locksmith, just ask for some they don't have any use for. Buy the same number of key tags, or make some yourself. Write your Mark's name and telephone number on the tag and mention ten dollar reward if found. After you've done this, drop them one by one around the city.

The drawback with this one is that you'll involve innocent third persons. A related trick would be to write your Mark's name and phone number on dollar notes.

Embarrassment

The best place to embarrass someone is to make it as public as possible. These tactics could look pretty innocent, but they will mostly feel like they were a hit below the belt for your casual shy Mark. The first one works best if your Mark is a shy homophobe, working in a store. Get a friend, someone your Mark doesn't know, to come into the store and buy a packet of condoms. Make him go to the Mark's line and say loudly, "I had a great time last night, (his name)

The Fine Art Of Getting Even

honey. Are these the kind you wanted me to pick up for later?" This scheme can naturally be adapted to other scenarios, and in several versions.

When your Mark is a younger brother it's even easier to embarrass him. Just ruin his reputation by running around at the school cafeteria asking for him saying that he forgot to bring his lunch with him. Dress geeky, smell and make sure you have a large grocery bag with his full name written on its side.

A different way to embarrass your Mark is if you're in gym class doing pushups. Have one of your trusted friends convince your Mark to ask you about how many push-ups your brother or sister can do.

When, the Mark asks, look as angry and upset as you can. Make a big scene out of it and give the Mark your response, "Who told you about this? How could you! You know my sister has no arms! What kind of person are you?!" At this point you can either storm out of the room or put your head down in your arms crying.

Using posters has always been one of my favorite ways of getting even. With the latest in technology (i.e. the campus PC's or your own) you can scan a picture of your Mark. The next thing you would need to do is go on the Net and find some pornographic images. You might have to search a little bit to find one that would fit nicely with your Mark's head, but it's well worth it. Cut and paste from the original picture, and smooth it together so that it looks real authentic.

Print it out and hang it on the campus display board with the text, "horny chick call XXX-XXXX."

The Fine Art Of Getting Even

Things that go boom!

I am not going to lecture anyone on
how to make hard explosives.
One reason is that there is enough
information on this around the Internet
already. Another is that explosives are
often unstable, and definitely
unreliable, which makes them

unsuitable for revenge. Not to mention the illegality!
There are still things you may "blow up" without
hurting anyone.
Take a balloon, fill it with paint and throw it onto
your Mark's car at a time when chances of detection
are lowest. The trick here is to find a balloon that will
hold the right amount of paint, and which will break
when it hits the car or house if you want to strike at
that.

Fun with frozen carbon dioxide

Dry ice (frozen CO_2) is cool and can be used to make
loud explosions. The way this is done, basically, is
that you put a generous amount of dry ice into a
bottle, lock the bottle and then hide it in the vicinity
of your Mark. Plastic bottles are recommended as
glass will break and may seriously hurt someone.

Fun with firecrackers

Firecrackers are also nice tools that can be used for
revenge purposes. Send a threatening note to your
Mark saying, "Tonight at 01:30AM, you die." Then at

night light the biggest firecracker you can find, just outside his house. This is psychological warfare. The next note could say, "Sorry, I missed."

Wreaking weddings

A wedding ceremony is both expensive and painstaking; the latter due to the somewhat difficult task of making everything look perfect.
Now, of course when our Mark is heading to the altar we'll be using this moment of vulnerability to get some serious revenge.

Showing up pregnant

Let's say this groom was an ex-lover of yours who ran away about 4-9 months prior to the wedding. After he ran away he abruptly fell in love with this little girl, who he proposed to and now is going to marry (yeah, right! he was cheating on you the whole time, this is a well-known scenario.) You feel that something has to be done, and to ruin our Mark's one-day-in-life you will need some pillows (or whatever) tucked under your sweater. After the ceremony you show up at the reception telling everybody about the forthcoming child of the groom.
This would certainly need some good acting, timing and realism. If you can leave the place without being exposed as a fraud (shouldn't be too hard), then I am sure the groom and bride's

wedding night isn't going to be very jolly.

Speaking up

Another dirty trick is to get into the church, watch the ceremony, waiting until the minister come to the part about "if there is anyone in this room who has anything to say about this marriage taking place." Okay, this stunt would also need quite a bit at guts, but for some, if that groom or the bride is an ex-lover you feel left some debt in the revenge department, then maybe getting up at this point, cussing out both the participants, wouldn't be too farfetched? The genius touch here is that nobody will shut you off. At the reception or at any time later there will be people who might yell back at you, but here in the church they won't.

A nice touch to this would maybe be to claim that you are already married to the groom/bride, and with luck you might prevent the couple from getting married that day. This might also lead to a nice night in jail for you, but that's a different story.

Photographs

A well-known urban story tells about a wedding where the groom (or bride) goes through the whole ceremony until the part where the commitment is about to take place. The groom then stops everyone and asks them to take a look at the picture

under their chair (church bench). The picture supposedly shows the bride in action with the best man the previous night. The groom then leaves the ceremony with another woman.

Epilogue / Also Known as the End

I've tried to focus on two things in particular in this book.

The implementation of various revenge schemes, and an elaboration on the worst pitfalls and how to secure your path around them on you mission of vengeance. It has not been my goal to write down every revenge scheme I could come up with, but rather describe a few of the more successful ones.

I hope that you, the reader, can use these as a source of inspiration in your quest, and that you can build on these rather than just copying them. The best revenge schemes are the ones which fit the crime, the Mark and his environment and you can't find that scheme in a book.

Another thing that you should be aware of is that the effort spent, doesn't always yield equal or justified agony for your Mark.

Imagine a person striving for hours plotting something that merely causes this Mark a few moments of discomfort, a situation that surely causes the avenger more agony than the Mark.

Revenge can also become an obsession, often seen in movies and books where the avenger, playing the bad guy, becomes obsessed with revenge and ruins both his own life and the life of the mark.

The line between revenge obsession and the psychotic is very indistinct.

The Fine Art Of Getting Even

Often people will find peace in their mind by imagining doing something to cause their Mark agony. Usually this seems to be enough, and it is definitely therapeutically.

The focus of a commitment should be to get a solution to a problem or an improvement of your situation, rather than just hurting your Mark.

Thinking revenge often solves the pain you may experience inside, without causing yourself or the Mark any harm.

I once heard that an ancient Chinese sage, or General or maybe just a laundryman once said that "He, who seeks to perform revenge on another, should dig two graves!" Or maybe, I just saw it in a fortune cookie, who knows, it doesn't matter the words ring true where ever they came from.

I hope this has been pleasant and entertaining reading. Have fun and be careful!

Printed in Great Britain
by Amazon